MW00560539

Written by Riley Preston

Text and illustration copyright © 2020 by Riley Preston

Published by Your Shift Matters Publishing,
a division of
Dana Zarcone International, LLC
www.DanaZarcone.com

Cover Design and Illustrations by
Prayan Animation Studio Pvt. Ltd.
www.prayananimation.com

Published in the United States
ISBN: 978-1-5136-6348-7

This book is dedicated to all the boys and girls out there,
helping to spread kindness everywhere.

Thank you to Ms. Jana for inspiring me to write this book.

To my Mom, who shows me that anything is possible.
Love you!

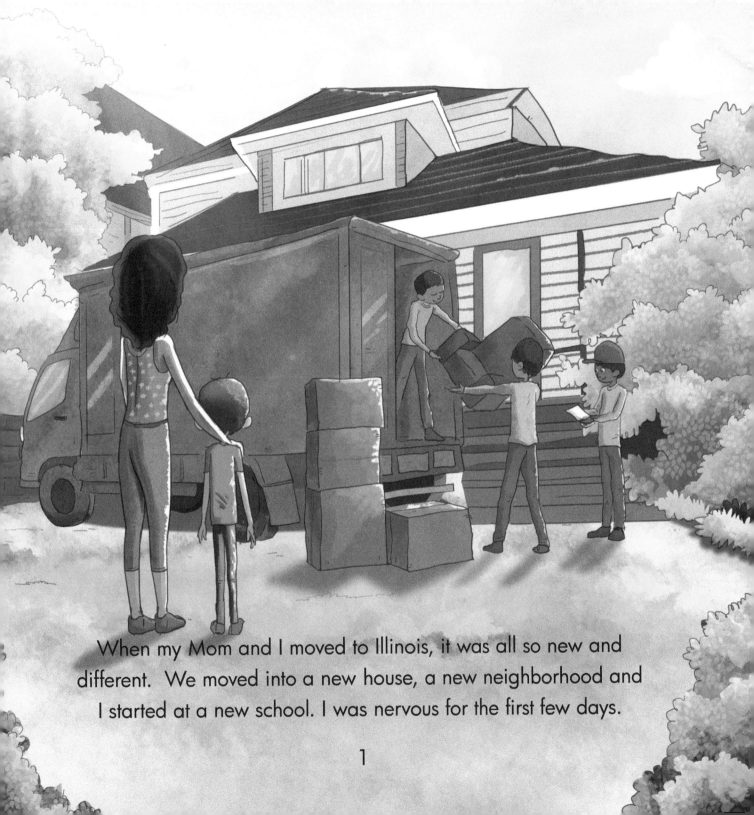

When my Mom and I moved to Illinois, it was all so new and different. We moved into a new house, a new neighborhood and I started at a new school. I was nervous for the first few days.

Some days were tough. I didn't have many friends, and at times, I was sad and lonely.

2

After school, I would talk to my Mom about the different things that happened and how I felt all alone.

My Mom told me that I might be uncomfortable at first.
She said that if I started talking to different kids and
offering to help others, I would start making friends.
She always makes me feel better.

4

I decided to give it a try, and here's what happened.

As I was walking to the bus stop, I saw Bella had dropped her book, so I picked it up and gave it back to her.

"Here you go, Bella. You dropped this." I said.
"Thank you for picking that up," she replied.

We continued to talk while we waited for the bus.
When the bus came, we decided to sit together.

Walking into school, I bumped into John.
"Hey John, I like your new shoes!"
"Thanks, Riley. I just got them. Aren't they cool?"

As we walked down the hallway to class, John spotted Megan,
who had a brightly colored dress on.
"I like the colors on your dress. It's really fun!"
"Thank you, John!"

10

They put their stuff in their lockers and hurried into the classroom just before the bell rang.

11

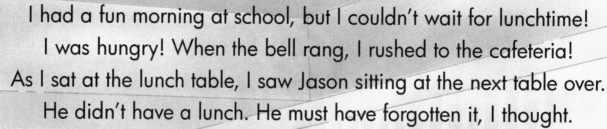

I had a fun morning at school, but I couldn't wait for lunchtime!
I was hungry! When the bell rang, I rushed to the cafeteria!
As I sat at the lunch table, I saw Jason sitting at the next table over.
He didn't have a lunch. He must have forgotten it, I thought.

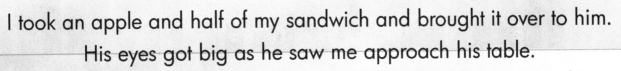

I took an apple and half of my sandwich and brought it over to him.
His eyes got big as he saw me approach his table.
He was so happy for the food that he had a huge grin on his face
as he said, "Thank you, I forgot my lunch at home."

After lunch, we all went outside for recess. Jason was all
smiles skipping out to the playground!
Then he noticed Susan struggling on the monkey bars.
"Can I help you, Susan?
I know a trick to make it easier, can I show you?"

14

"I keep falling and can't seem to keep my balance. It would be great if you could help me. Thank you!"
Jason showed her his trick, and Susan was able to make it across the monkey bars. She was so excited!

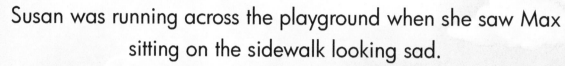

Susan was running across the playground when she saw Max
sitting on the sidewalk looking sad.
"Hey, Max. What's going on?"
Max said, "I don't have anyone to play catch with."
"I'll play catch with you!"

16

They played catch until the bell rang,
and it was time to head back to class.
After school, we all headed to after school care!

We were playing outaside, and Max noticed
Joanna was playing by herself.
"Joanna, would you like to play foursquare?"
"Sure! That sounds like a lot of fun! Let's go play."

As they finished their foursquare game, Joanna noticed
a boy sitting by himself.
She walked over to him and said, "my name is Joanna. What's
your name?" "My name is Tyler."
"Do you want to be friends?" Joanna said.

"That would be nice. I don't have many friends here. I'm new."
Joanna and Tyler went off to play in the gym together. There was a game
of dodgeball going on, so they asked if they could join. The other kids
welcomed them to the game! They were both so excited to play.
After the game, everyone was hungry, so they went
to the snack shack to buy snacks.

20

Tyler saw that Jessie was standing towards the back, "are you going to get a snack?" Jessie replied, "I don't have any money." "I have one dollar," Tyler said. "I will split it with you so that you can get a snack too." "Thank you, Tyler. I'm so hungry."
Jessie was all smiles and went to sit with the other kids eating their snacks.

By the next day, we were all good friends, and I learned that one small act of kindness could make a huge difference!

YOU can make a huge difference!
Help us spread kindness EVERYWHERE!

23